AF572010

5 SMOOTH STONES

JOANN KLUSMEYER

Copyright © 2020 by Joann Klusmeyer

All rights reserved. This book or any portion thereof may not be reproduced or transmitted in any form or manner, electronic or mechanical, including photocopying, recording, or by any information storage or retrieval system, without the express written permission of the copyright owner except for the use of brief quotations in a book review or other noncommercial uses permitted by copyright law.

Printed in the United States of America

Library of Congress Control Number: 2020920839
ISBN: Softcover 978-1-64908-477-4
eBook 978-1-64908-476-7

Republished by: PageTurner Press and Media LLC
Publication Date: 10/21/2020

To order copies of this book, contact:

PageTurner Press and Media
Phone: 1-888-447-9651
order@pageturner.us
www.pageturner.us

5 SMOOTH STONES

Selected stepping stones through the bible, set in rhyme.

FIVE SMOOTH STONES

A small, smooth stone.
Its color glowing softly in the flow.
To look at it and wonder…who would know?
That it was chosen… it alone.

A rushing brook?
A firey mass… a crackling lava flow.
Great upheaval..starting deeply from below…
Was what it took.

A tiny crack.
The desert cold, the scorching noonday heat…
A rushing multitude of small, hoofed feet.
With no relief.

A crumbling edge.
The beating rain… the dusty desert wind…
More breaking of the stone, to send it
Reeling from the ledge.

It was a start.
The boulder cracked apart and crumbled.
Loud! Like hail on stone, it shattered.. rumbled
And broke apart.

Soon it must go.
A tumbling, rushing journey looms ahead.
They roll together in the small stream bed,
The pebbles flow.

As fate would be,
Some stones are trampled in the ground
Never to be sculptured smooth and round.
Just more debris.

The stones move on.
Some stones will fall beneath the flow
And there remain. Buried, they will never know
Where life has gone.

And still they move.
A valley lies between two mountain sides
It's where a round, smooth rolling stone abides.
No moving on.

No chip or crack.
Just the smoothness made by wear,
And restless friction caused by getting there.
...Victim of the pack.

So rest and wait.
There's one important duty left to do.
A broken chip of stone will not aim true.
That is its fate.

So it must be
It takes a stone of flint to make a spark.
It takes a smooth, hard stone to hit its mark.
When it's set free!

Stay standing steady.
It's not a bad thing to be found
The one who's worn and tossed around.
It doesn't mean you might be losing ground.
Only.....
...That when the Slinger's hand is wound
Stone in the sling goes round and round...
... you will be ready!

... And he took his staff in his hand, and chose him five smooth stones out of the brook, and put them in a shepherd's bag which he had... 1 Samuel 17:40

IT ISN'T THE SIZE, BUT THE PURPOSE

It isn't the length of the strap on the sling
It's the size of the stone in the pocket.

It isn't the point of the hardest of steel
It's the blast that's the power of the rocket.

It isn't the words as they fill up a book,
It always needs someone to read it.

Nothing is learned by a quick, fleeting look
But a thought with a good word to lead it.

It isn't the words that say, "I love you, God."
Then live out a life without changin'.

It's works of obedience, actions of love
To show that life's had rearrangin'.

…And Samuel said unto Jesse, "Are (these) here all thy children? And he said, ":There remaineth yet the youngest…"

NOTE: For the entire story of how a boy was anointed king, see 1 Samuel chapter 16.

WHAT'S FOR SUPPER?

"What's for supper?
"Adam's tired of everything I fix.
"Just something different…
"Surely there's a new taste in this mix."

"It's Eden's Garden!
"Sure it's lovely, at least that's what I hear.
"But here's a fact.
"For my life long I've always had it here."

"What is 'weary'?
"I've never done a thing I didn't want to do."
"What is 'ugly'?
"I only know this garden…
"Who are you?"

A STRANGER

Smooth as silk…
The voice came from a low branch of the tree.
"My daughter, listen…
"I have the answerhere for you. Hark to me.

"The tree of knowledge…
"I know God said that you must never touch.
"For there's a reason…
"It means God doesn't like you very much."

THE WOMAN

"Oh, you're mistaken!
"God's love and care is growing all around!
"It's all I ever wished for,
"Growing up around me from the ground."

THE STRANGER

Came the soft words…
"Yet you stand still looking, watching for the things you cannot get.
"It's you, my friend…
"It's you who are mistaken. That tree holds for you the answer, yet..
"Did not God say…
"The fruit of that tree holds the knowledge of all life?"
"You stand and look…
'Your thoughts of longing slash you like a knife."
"That's what God wants.
"He made you long for all the knowledge that ever was.
"I know you well…
"You long to know each reason, every 'why' and every "cause'"

THE WOMAN

And still she stood.
How could this lovely creature know her well?
He speaks the truth…
How can he know the thoughts I cannot tell?

THE STRANGER

Again he spoke.
"It's here, my friend. You must only lift your lovely hand
"And take the fruit.
"You'll have all the knowledge of the world that you command."

SO THEN

She reached and plucked.
The tender fruit dropped lightly in her hand.
She took a bite
And things she never dreamed, she now could understand.

"Come quickly, Adam.
"Come try this fruit. God did not tell us it would taste so good."
"A small mistake, though
"God surely meant for us to have this food."

She chewed and swallowed.
The fruit became a part… A particle within her………
The fruit was lovely!
Then they knew the truth. The lovely beast had lied!"

THE LYING STRANGER

He left them, laughing…
No longer lovely on his limb, he crawled the dust.
With words of beauty…
He'd lied to every human when he made them trust.

In Eden's Garden…
The weight of evil in the world
The frightened humans…
Now knew much more! They knew a lot they'd never wished to know.

God sighed in heaven.
The humans that He loved now knew the truth of sin.
And ever after…
That bit of sin would live and grow, and multiply within.

And now God knew…
As He had always known, that evil knowledge now would be a part
Of every creature.
Old Lucifer now knew the way to every human heart.

There was one way.
The only hope for humans, now, was God, Himself, within
To combat evil.
His Word became His loved and only Son.

The time would come.
Yes, time would come. A pure and sinless body must be born.
Of flesh and blood.
Yes, time would come. The pure and sinless body would be torn!

So take and eat…
This Body torn and broke will make you sinless… new!
"Here is the answer.
"I die to let you live… it's what I came to earth to do.

"It was your choice.
"You freely took the fruit now it's become a part of you.
"Another choice, now,
"To take of me. Another choice, my child, and freely up to you."

"It was your choice.
"You stubbornly refused to listen to my Word.
"It was your choice.
"It was a trick, but still it's up to you chose

"It was My choice.
"My body's broken, and here is what that fact can mean for you.
"It is your choice.
"As far is east is from the west, I'll take the sin from you,
"The Sea of Forgetfulness!
"Never to be seen again by you!"

NOTE: For background see Genesis Chapter 2 and John Chapter 19.

THE SYCAMORE TREE

The Sycamore tree. By the wayside. Nothing special or unique.
Not one to be remembered, or inspire words to speak.
(But a man who was quite small
Climbed it… then was tall.)
And then through limbs and leaves, he took a peek.

Who was this famous Man? He was sure that, without doubt,
This was the Man of Whom there was such talk about!
His avid, curiosity was such
That he must see… and maybe touch
This man. Far ahead, down on the way, he heard a shout.

Around the bend, he heard a crowd, a noisy patter
Feet pounding on the path, excited voices chatter.
Small man crowded closer, bolder
He saw elbow, ear and shoulder.
His nimble brain thought quickly what to do about the matter.

The Sycamore tree! Tall and solid. Nothing special, not at all
Yet it was close, and there it stood so straight and tall.
Small man climbed above the crowd,
And though the voices were still loud…
He looked down at the Man, and clearly heard His call…

"Come down! For you're the man I really came to see.
Today I dine with you, and you will dine with Me."
Now, who is there to really say
Would that have happened anyway…
Without the tree? Maybe, but I like to think it was the key.

Then I thought…

Lord, if You've no special plan or duty just for me,
Sycamore tree!

Now that is something I might like to be.
Just a tree with limbs in place,
To help another see Thy Face.
Just a tree to help another look at Thee?
Could I be just someone
To share a glimpse of Thee?

… And he ran before, and climbed up into a sycamore tree to see (Jesus) for he was to pass that way. Luke 19:4

NOTE: For the complete story of the short man, Zacchaeus, see Luke 19:1-10

WATER ON THE GROUND

Parched throats… and dusty. Dry as flint.
Dirt clods scuffed at soldiers dragging feet.
Chased like a partridge on a meadow
Eating what they found that they could eat.

Loyal followers… friends, protectors.
Rugged men who knew him well
Gathering round, they reassured him,
Him… the future King of Israel

Like snarling wolves protecting young ones!
Fought before their mountain den.
David's army loved and served him.
Closer than a brother they had been.

Like a skip flea in the desert
Royal army's swords are in each hand.
All the band of King Saul's army
Waiting poised for his command.

Parched throats sought the water.
Dry as dust within the dell
Royal army round them guarded,
Will not let them reach the well.

"Oh, for one more drink of water."
David moaned in tired voice.
Two friends paused. They thought.
Their eyes met. Quickly made their choice.

Bravely through Saul's standing army
Like a serpent through the grass…
From tree to rock and past the soldiers
Silent as a breeze, they pass.

Filled the bottle from the water
Gushing from his favorite well
This they could do, he was their leader
Pride within began to swell.

Back they crept, like breezes whisper,
Through the army of the king.
Bottle filled with ....water!
Was the least that they could bring.

David gazed upon the bottle
Held in hand, now battle scared.
Gazed upon his two friends' bravery.
Then gazed to heaven... eyes tear-marred.

In amazement, soldiers staring
Water pouring on the ground.
Then no drop still in the bottle,
Just a damp spot on the ground.

"My dear friends, words cannot tell you.
"What this water meant to me.
"I wished a gift for God, our Father
"But here within my hands I see...

"Like a hind through fields of lions...
"Like a bird through raging flame...
"I know what this water cost you.
"Years from now they'll know your name."

"Comrades, brave, with sword and buckler
"Took your place, and soldiered well.
"They will also share in God's favor
"That the future voices tell."

"Sacrifice has many wrappings.
"Gifts of labor, gifts are laid.
"Gifts unnoticed, kind words uttered
"Never expect to be repaid."

If no price is paid, no risk attached?
What is the meaning... sacrifice?
What is the meaning of true giving?
Answer? It's a gift that costs a price.

...And the three mighty men brake through the host of the Philistines and drew water out of the well of Bethlehem, that was by the gate, and took it, and brought it to David: nevertheless he would not drink thereof, nut poured it out unto the Lord.

NOTE: For the story of a sacrifice given to David, and David's sacrifice to God, see II Samuel 23: 12-17

THE DAY A RAVIN CROWED

I don't like it here!
I know I'm just a raven but I know that I'm not free.
Or so it seems to me.

That open window
I see the days of rain have finally gone. The sky is blue.
I dream of flying through.

The hand could loose me.
I'd leave this perch and through the upper window fly!
My lovely mate and I…

I stand here longing.
Tethered to this perch, a place I've come to purely hate.
Here by my lovely mate.

No! He picked the dove!
On pale white wings she rose and now she's gone forevermore.
Fly fast and free… explore!

Just my mate and I.
We are only two… and of the doves, they number seven.
One flies to heaven.

Feet on the window.
She's back! Her weak and flimsy wings are needing rest.
No place for her to nest.

That open window…
If Noah picked me, I'd go up and up on strongest wing.
My open beak would sing!

Up through the window.
A chance to stretch my wings… a chance to fly and fly!
My lovely mate and I!

Oh, no! The dove again!
He thrust her through the window. Wings flap as she flies high.
A light speck in the sky.

But look! She's fluttered back.
There in her beak she holds a green and leafy branch.
She's missed her chance!

I hate this floating prison.
My mate is droopy. Lovely feathers floating to the floor.
I fear she'll grow no more.

Oh, my tether's loosened!
Hands lift me upward. I feel my feathers shiver with delight.
Wings aching for a flight!

Up through the window!
Water everywhere! Tips of green pierce gaily through the wave.
Wings must behave.

I cannot wander
Without my mate. I'll circle round and round this ugly boat
How can such a prison float?

Mate still within.
I wait and sigh. I want to be the first thing she will see,
When she flies free.

The boat is resting!
And there's a tree so tall. Sturdy limbs surround a lovely nesting site.
To give my mate delight.

I perch here waiting.
I watch the crawling, marching prisoners as they onward go.
Flying high or plodding slow.

The man is waiting.
Gazing here and there. Where will the prisoned people go?
Why is my mate so slow?

And there she is!
Her tired wings flap slowly, climbing into flight.
She turns each way… eyes wide and searching, building height.
And now she sees me! Gaining new strength by the sight!
Now all is right!

What will people do?
Who cares? not I! My mate and I will start our life anew.
That would be a ravin thing to do!

…..And it came to pass at the end of forty days, that Noah opened the window of the ark which he had made: and he sent forth a raven, which went forth to and fro, until the waters were dried up off the earth. Genesis 8: 6-7

NOTE: For the complete story of Noah;s time on the ark, see Genesis 8: 1-20

NO ROOM IN THE INN? NONSENSE!

Mary riding on a donkey?
 Well, it could have been a cart.
Anyway, the trip was surely made
 With Nazareth as it's start.

Their gold and silver came along.
 The family came in style.
Joseph was a working man…
 Perhaps they'd stay a while.
Bethlehem could use the help
 He decided with a smile.

Bethlehem had many jobs.
 The mom and Babe could use the rest.
They'd visit kin and see the world.
 They'd be the city's guest.
They'd pay old Herod's taxes
 For that they'd made this quest.
He'd given the matter careful thought
 And that plan seemed the best.

They'd spend the first night at the inn,
 Then he'd find a place to rent.
His Mary's precious burden……
 Was clearly heaven sent.
So, if he did the best he could
 He'd have to be content.
For, Joseph did the best he could,
 But didn't have a hint…
He couldn't know the change of plans
 Would be no accident.

The city streets were crowded
 From the roadbed to each door.

Nose to elbow, toe to heel
They'd not hold any more.
Searching for a place to stay,
Would be a tiresome chore.
He pushed on to the nearest inn,
Exhausted, dusty and footsore.
While Mary waited in the street
He looked the situation 'ore.
He really didn't have a choice
But pushed on as before.

He sought the keeper of the inn.
He then came face to face, as
The keeper sadly shook his head.
No where was there a place.
The room for them, so crowded,
And it surely was the case
The place for keeping moms and babes
Was smelly… noisy! A disgrace!
To leave his Mary in that room
Would have been hard to face.
While Joseph stood, he saw the truth
His mind could not erase.
A good idea, the keeper had,
"Sir, there just might be a place."

"Of course" thought tired Joseph.
"This spacc could bc thc onc.
'Of course the Heavenly Father
"Saved a place to birth his Son."
Though Joseph's careful planning
Would occasionally come undone,
God's will would be accomplished.
Of mistakes, there would be none.

So with the quiet cattle sighs
The Baby's life begun, and
The rules surround the Babe
Were provided by Someone.

The very heavens opened and
The angel's song was sung.
The world would speak with fear and awe
Of earth's and heaven's....
.... Wonderous great Phenomenon!

... And she brought forth her first-born son, and wrapped him in swaddling clothes, and laid him in a manger: because there was no room for them in the inn. Luke 2:7

NOTE: For the complete story of Christmas, see Luke, Chapter 2

FIRE IN THE SKY

A flaming chariot through the sky!
With stretching neck and blinking eye;
 Who would ever think to see
 A sight like this? Perchance to be
Where such a sight as this came passing by?

What harm is there to take a look?
...Was just a moment that it took
 To see the marvelous flaming wheels!
 Surely, this, God's power reveals!
I say... what harm to take a look!

Elisha wanted double power.
He knew he neared the final hour...
 The time his teacher would be gone.
 And then he would be left alone.
He needed... needed... all that extra power.

His teacher said, You will receive
The gift you want, if, when I leave
 Your eyes are on me. Never waver.
 That is how you'll get your favor.
It won't be easy, friend, you must believe."

Elisha stuck to him like glue.
This was a thing that he could do.
 He hardly let his eyelids blink.
 He had no other thought to think,
He knew that he must somehow see this trial through.

And when that fateful day came by,
A fiery chariot filled up the sky.
 He knew this was his only chance...
 And did not risk one single glance...

The flaming horses galloped by the corner of his eye.

Then whirlwind came, and round and round,
His master left, in wind and sound.
  Elisha's eyes trained on the sky.
  He saw his master's last goodbye,
The gift of power and robe came floating down.

What lesson for the world today?
Elisha'a words might go this way.
  "Obey! Obey! Obey! Obey!"
  What left is there for him to say?
Except, once more, "Watch and obey!"

…and behold there appeared a chariot of fire, and horses of fire, and parted them both asunder, and Elijah went up by a whirlwind into heaven. II Kings 2: 11

NOTE: for the whole story of Elisha's gift of twice as much power as Elijah, see II Kings 2: 9-14

THE MARY – MARTHA SYNDROME

I'd rather be a mountain stream
  Than be a silent pool.
My mind keeps seeking movement
  Making that my daily rule.

I can look with puzzled glance
  At folks still sitting on their duff,
Not doing things that could be done
  While there's still time enough.

As years began to settle down
  Like soft clouds made of mist,
I can look at empty arms
  And contemplate closed fists,
And see there's nothing I have done
  That I can really hold as mine…
That much has passed my actions, just
  Like bubbles pass through wine.

I see the fading footprints where
  I moved across time's soil.
I see the times I helped to "build"…
  And times I was the "spoil'.
I splashed along, stroke after stroke
  And never stopped to note
That I was swimming fiercely when
  I could be in the boat.

I came to earth when motorcars
  Rolled smoothly on 4 wheels.
I lived to see the rocket's burst
  And flames scorch foreign fields,
And satellites above the clouds
  Like eagles without wings…

While cameras dredge the ocean depth
And weave through Saturn's rings.

Like Martha, as the story goes,
Preparing things to eat
While Mary sought eternal things
Before the Master's feet.

Higher, faster hurls the earth
As planets always will,
And not a thing on earth is changed
Had I been standing still.

…Martha was cumbered about much serving, and came to (Jesus) and said, :Lord, dost thou not care that my sister hath left me to serve alone? Bid her therefore that she come and help me.

And Jesus answered and said unto her, Martha! Martha! Thou art careful and troubled about many things: but one thing is needful and Mary hath chosen that good part, which shall not be taken away from her. Luke 10: 40-42

IS THAT YOU, LORD?

"Is that you, Lord?
A bush of flame just came to be!
With only desert sand to see,
Your flames came crackling suddenly."

"Is that you, Lord?"
Have you come to punish me
For sins that only you can see?
Is there no place where I can be?"

"Is that you, Lord?"
"Yes, I'm right here in that crackling sound.
You thought you'd hide and not be found
But you stand now on holy ground."

"Really you, Lord?"
"My child, I tracked you day and night
Until the perfect time was right
And you'd developed strength of might."

"Oh, no, my Lord,
A craven, trembling coward. Fast I ran
I left behind a buried man.
Lord, You've forgotten who I am!"

"And there's more, Lord.
Have you forgotten how I stutter…
Struggle with each word I utter?
I can't put one word 'ore the other."

Reply came down.
"I see your inner will is strong.
I saw you try to right a wrong.
I brought you here where you belong.

"If you could speak with words of gold
You would be proud, and then, behold!
You would not do as you were told.

"I brought you here to tend the flock
On scorching sand and bruising rock
So you will listen when I talk.

"I taught you patience day by day.
To learn of Me, you had a mother.
For golden words, you had a brother.
Your sister watched you like no other.

"You were as a cake half baked.
I knew your teachings… you'd forsake,
Then you would see your grave mistake.

"I brought you here so you would know
I always knew that you speak slow
You were born high…I brought you low.
I shaped and molded you… just so…
So go, my child and tell Pharoah,
That God said, "Let my people go!"

What more could Moses say or do
Except "Yes, Lord, that's you!"

…And the angel of the Lord appeared unto him in a flame of fire out of the midst of a bush: and he looked, and behold, the bush burned with fire and the bush was not consumed. Exodus 3: 2

NOTE: For the story of Moses' calling by God to lead his people out of Egypt, see Exodus 3: 1-22

BUT WHAT ABOUT THE RAVENS?

Elijah went in hiding,
Waiting for God's perfect plan.

The map for plans of action
Started when the earth began.

What about the ravins,
Where were they, that day?

Were they waiting by the brook
When the prophet came to stay?

Did they ever get impatient?
Maybe try to fly away?

What if Elijah didn't come?
Then what were they to do?

While they brought Elijah's food,
Did they get hungry, too?

Or did they, maybe, get a share…
Part of the prophet's bread?

One thing is sure and certain
God would see the birds were fed.

How did the ravens carry food?
Did one bird carry meat?

I wonder how they managed…
How to keep it fit to eat.

I wonder how they held it…
With claws, or in the beak?

And bread… it mustn't crumble
And end up splashing in the creek!

Then what kind of meat… I wonder?
Did it learn to be a thief?

And know where some rich merchant
Was, that moment, carving beef?

Also… was it cooked or raw?
Was it "economy"… or "prime"?

Elijah could have cooked it.
He certainly had the time.

Unless the smoke of cooking fire
Would betray his hiding place.

Or would God send a twisting wind
To make the rising smoke erase.

How many birds were on the job?
When did they get a break?

Or maybe God gave extra strength,
When they would fly in with a steak?

How did the ravens always know
When it was time for lunch?

Did they always have a schedule?
Or would they just obey a hunch?

Or did they rob a housewife's fire?
The bread would then be very fresh.

And did the birds who brought the meat
Also sometimes dive for fish?

Or did the fish jump on the bank
To let themselves be caught.

Fish were known to obey God.
We know they can be taught.
(just ask Jonah)

… hide thyself by the brook Cherith that is there by Jordan. And it shall be that thou shalt drink of the brook, and I have commanded the ravens to feed thee there. I Kings 17: 2-3

NOTE: The story of his stay at the brook, see I Kings 17: 1-9

A QUESTION OF BREAD AND MEAT

Elijah went in hiding waiting
For God's perfect plan.
(The plan of action started
'Ere the time the earth began.)

It started out with Adam,
Then Noah took his place.
Abraham came on the scene
And met God face to face.

There was Jacob and his ladder
Joseph was his favorite son.
He had dreams about the future
And about the time to come.

After that there came Elijah,
Boldly standing for God's words.
There came a time he must be hidden
By a brook, and fed by birds

BUT WHAT ABOUT THE RAVENS?

Were they waiting by the brook
When the prophet came to stay?

Did they ever get impatient?
Maybe try to fly away?

What if Elijah didn't come?
What then were they to do?

While they brought Elijah's food,
Did they get hungry, too?

Or did they, maybe, get a share…
Part of the prophet's bread?

One thing is for sure and certain
God would see the birds were fed.

How did the ravens carry food?
Did one bird carry meat?

I wonder how they managed…
How to keep it fit to eat.

I wonder how they held it…
With claws, or in the beak?

And bread… it mustn't crumble
And end up splashing in the creek!

Then what kind of meat… I wonder?
Raven learns to be a thief?

And know where some rich merchant
Was, that moment, carving beef?

Also… was it cooked or raw?
Was it "economy"… or "prime"?

Elijah could have cooked it.
He certainly had the time.

Unless the smoke of cooking fire
Would betray his hiding place.

Or would God send a twisting wind
To make the rising smoke erase.

How many birds were on the job?
When did they get a break?

Or maybe God gave extra strength,
When they would fly in with a steak?

How did the ravens always know
When it was time for lunch?

Did they always have a schedule?
Or would they just obey a hunch?

Or did they rob a housewife's fire?
The bread would then be very fresh.

And did the birds who brought the meat
Also sometimes dive for fish?

Or did the fish jump on the bank
To let themselves be caught.

Fish were known to obey God.
We know they can be taught.
(just ask Jonah!)

I don't know how long Elijah
Stayed there by the Cherith brook.

Another thing I sometimes wonder, is,
Just how many birds it took?

Or if, when birds were growing older
Were their new replacements trained?

And did they search a new supply source
When an older source was drained?

So many stories in the Good Book
Leave some details there to ponder.

Just how the stories all turned out…
There are times it makes me wonder.

I know, for sure, there'll come a time
When everything will be made plain.

No question or detail from earth
  Or from the heaven will remain .

I know all of that for certain but I really must admit
I sit with coffee at McDonalds, with my patience and my wit,
And when that blessed time arrives,
          I will not care one tiny bit!

...Get thee hence and turn thee eastward, hide thyself by the brook, Cherith, that is before Jordan. And it shall be that thou shalt drink of the brook and I have commanded the ravens to feed thee there," I Kings 17: 3-4

NOTE: The details around this event in the life of Elijah are found in I Kings 17: 1-8

JOB, REWARD UNFINISHED

There was a time when Satan talked to God
and made the strangest bargain in the Book.
"God, I know you think Job loves You for Yourself.
in spite of wealth and family that I took.

"If you would only let me touch his life,
You'll find that he will curse You to Your face.
God said, 'Then do it! You'll see what Job
will do to put you in your place…"

So Satan did…
"You're miserable! Just curse your God and die!"
These words were harshly uttered by his mate.
With running sores, Job sat in poverty,
And even dogs felt sorry for his fate.

Of course God won the wager. When He did,
He gifted Job with good in every way.
God let Job live his life in comfort… peace,
and Satan had to skulk and walk away.

What about us…
Just when we think that everything is gone,
that everything in life has turned out wrong,
Think! There just might be wager about you,
God proudly telling Satan you are strong!

Now, Job was much rewarded on the earth
That's just one way to show what God's about.
It may not happen just that way for you
But faith will be rewarded, never doubt.

Think BIG! Our God is great and mighty,
So nothing that He ever does is small.

There WILL be gifts God has prepared for you.
So your reward may be so
BIG and WIDE and TALL…
So rich in wealth, it must be held for you in heaven…
Perhaps old earth can't hold it after all!

… This is the story of Job, when God made a wager with the devil. Job, Chapter 1

EARS, EYES AND FEET

Peter's ears could hear the word,
His faith was soaring free.
His brain knew Jesus had the power
When He said "Come to me."
But Peter's eyes saw rolling waves
His feet sank in the sea.

"Lord, save me lest I perish!"
Peter's anxious call rang out.
Peter's feet sank ever lower
As waves rolled all about.
His eyes turned from his power
And his brain was filled with doubt.

Then Peter saw the Master's hand
His doubts were cast aside.
Faith conquered weakness as the Touch
Lifted him from out the tide.
Train eyes on Christ. The best advice
Works miracles each time it's tried.

Ears are made to hear a word
And a brain is made to know.
Feet are made to travel in
The way that's right to go.
Though Peter looked for fishes,
It was Jesus that he saw.

Peter saw his Master's feet.
Stepped firmly on the wave.
Peter knew it would be Christ
Who made the sea behave.
"Master bid me come to you."
"Come" was the answer Jesus gave.

…Peter answered… and said, “Lord, if it be thou, bid me come unto thee on the water.” And (Jesus) said, “Come.” Matthew 14: 28-29

NOTE: For the story of the storm at sea, see Matthew 14:22-33

WHEN IN DOUBT...(trust your horse)

STOLEN! The Ark of Israel was GONE!
Over hills and through the valleys. Then BEYOND!

The thief decided…

"That must be where their God Lives.
The God who feeds and fights their wars.
Now we can get the gifts It gives!"
We'll steal it from the place it lives!

It didn't work that way. But why?
"We told the ark. We thought it heard,
Exactly what we bade it do.
But I don't think It heard a word."

"Bad luck. That's all we've had from it.
Trouble! Triple trouble! Take it back!
Or find the words to make it work.
This can't go on… and that's a fact."

Answer…

Old man said, "Let's pose a riddle.
We'll take two kine who've given birth.
Hitch to the wagon, turn them loose.
That way we'll see what words are worth."

Wagon and the Ark were brought in.
The two cows stomped impatiently.
They heard their babies hungry bawl….
As they hitched to the wagon tree.

Buckles tightened. Workerswent away.
An instant, and cows began to race.
Galloping, bawling, to Israel's camp
Astonished look on each watcher's face.

The cows knew where the Ark belonged.
But could this be a one-time thing?
Not hardly! Think of the prophet who
Took money from Israel's enemy king.

"Just curse those folks! As you know how!
I know you know just what to do.
Curse them! Bring them evil luck,
And I will give much gold to you."

So Balaam on his mule, strode out
To earn the king's corrupted gold.
His 'stubborn' donkey shied away
And bluntly would not do as told.

Balaam struck the poor beast's back.
His greedy guilt was coming clear.
He knew God's power, but did not heed.
The pull of gold was far more dear.

When greedy Balaam would not stop,
The donkey scraped against a rock
And crushed his rider's dangling leg.
God gave the donkey voice to talk.

"Why do you beat me? Can't you see
The angel standing in my way?
I can't go forward on the road
No matter what you do or say!"

What next?

Two great thoughts could come of this.
When in doubt, with puzzles, reason…
Speak to the animal close to you,
And let your dog make the decision.

Or…..

I'd hand the puzzle back to God,
And wait with prayer to know His choice.
Wait! Even puzzles have solutions.
Seek a way to hear God's voice.

I hope I never have to
hear my Buick speak!

This is a light hearted version of the account when the Ark of God was stolen ,(1 Samuel 4:11) and the way the cows brought it back. (1 Samuel Chapter 6) And also the account of the talking donkey (Numbers 22: 5-41)

MY OWN THEORY

In long ago history
There lies a true mystery.
How the earth was created… a puzzling thought.
It could have been quickly,
It's crust forming thickly.
Or maybe a mass of despicable rot.

Or maybe a spin
With an unearthly din
As the earth ball went hurling through eons of space.
Or primly and pert
Stacking layers of dirt
Till the whole thing was formed over time, in one place.

Or a soggy morass…
An explosion of gas
That would instantly form like the mist of a cloud.
And the tall mountains, soon,
Like a mammoth balloon,
Stood tall on the landscape, all purple and proud.

Or a crash and a tumble,
An almighty rumble
Found its parts slammed together with all things in one place
Like the wings of a gnat
And the tongue of a bat
And the sprinkle of freckles decorating a face.

But the one thing I know,
Be it fast---be it slow,
However the method…however the way…
What the elements heard
Was the sound of God's word
With His verbal instructions to water and clay.

Could be daytime or night,
Words like, "Let there be light!"
His words chose the place and the very best time.
When his words died away,
In the space of a day,
The world was complete like the words of this rhyme.

This is a light-hearted account of how the world was created. (Genesis Chapter 1)

TWO MULES' BURDEN OF DIRT

Proud and haughty, stiff and prim…
Soldiers bowed their heads to him
And fiercely fought and stood with pride
So gratefully, joyfully by his side.

Namaan was the very best
At what he did. He did not rest
(Until he saw the spot of white,
Shine like a beacon in the light.)

Doctors worked to no avail.
The leper spot stayed ghostly pale.
When Namaan could no longer hide,
He sought help from the enemy's side.

The answer came the strangest way.
Here's what Elisha had to say,
"Go to River Jordan's side,
Dip seven times beneath the tide."

Namaan looked with hate… disgust!
He was so angry! Must he trust…
In Jordan's muddy depth to heal
The pale and painful, widening weal?

The river, roiling with spring tide,
Outflowed the bank on either side..
"Why should I take a bath right here…
With Syria's river's clean and pure?"

But desperate Namaan swallowed pride
And ducked 'neath Jordan's muddy tide.
He bowed down in the river's bed
As water closed above his head.

He shook the water from his hair
And stared. The white spot was not there.
The skin was pink, he saw with joy,
As when he was a little boy!

Now he was coming home again!
He wore his miracle of new skin
And saw his enemy in this way,
For here is what he had to say....

"Get me mules... a wagon strong...
Fill it with dirt and don't be long!
This hated country set me free
A part of it goes home with me!"

THE END...BUT YET...

I think I know what happened next.
That Namaan's wife was sorely vexed.
She saw the two mule's pack of dirt
Her nimble mind became alert.

"His brand, new skin is such to see…
Why would that mud not work for me?
I'll try a bit of Namaan's dirt.
He's well again, what could it hurt?

"With Israel's mud pack on my face,
Would spots and wrinkles then erase?
And I'd be perfect once again
With soft and lovely brand new skin"

Think a bit. Who's here to say
That story did not go that way?
New skin for what was old and worn…
The "mud pack" could…
…have just been born!

;;;And Naaman said, "Shall there not then, I pray thee, be given to thy servant two mules' burden of earth" For they servant will henceforth offer neither burnt offering nor sacrifice to other gods, but unto the Lord. II Kings 5: 17

NOTE: This is the story of Naaman's unusual cure from leprosy, account described in the whole fifth chapter.

THE BARLEY CAKE

Barley. A common grass for any soil. Sunshine and a little rain, and just a bit of toil, would grow sustaining food that could be hidden. (Now that proper fields had been forbidden.)

The enemy, like locusts in the land, took every fertile field they could command, while Israel cried to God in agony, "God, send to us a man to set us free."

To Gideon, in his hidden field of grain, a shining man proceeded to explain, "God saw beyond the wine press… you were there, so you will be the answer to your People's prayer."

BUT GIDEON SAID…

"Oh, no! A grave mistake. A humble farmer, you can see. It would be a grave mistake if God chose me! Sir, my old father and the men who came before, bowed as they tilled the ground, and nothing more."

WHAT HAPPENED

The story tells about the fleece and dew, how Gideon tried to think whathe should do. It talks about how, hiding by a tent, he heard about the dream God must have sent.

THE DREAM OF THE ENEMY

"I dreamed a barley cake rolled down the hill. Destroyed our tents. The dream gave me a chill!" His nodding friend said, "Yes, and here's my take. That farmer, Gideon, he's the barley cake. I feel there's something new with Israelites. They claim to have a God who wins their fights!"

When Gideon and friend heard that remark, the truth came down like lightening in the dark. Gideon's army was pathetic, weak and small. Most were quivering cowards, after all.

But God said, "Gideon, you have far too many men. I'm sending you to battle. You will win. This army must not say, when war is won, 'Just look at all the great things WE have done!"

So God began to whittle men away. Three hundred were all He allowed to stay. The battle happened in the dark of night and Midianites ran screaming in their fright.

Many sermons base upon this text. One would be, "Don't worry what comes next." With God in charge, there is no need for men.

Many lessons hide within this story. When God works, He must get the glory. Just ask Moses, Jonah, Gideon… it's not odd. There's no use arguing against God!

…And when Gideon was come, behold, there was a man that told a dream unto his fellow, and said, "Behold, I dreamed a dream, and, lo, a cake of barley bread tumbled into the host of Midian, and came that it unto a tent, and smote that it fell, and overturned it, that they tent lay along.

NOTE: Several chapters tell of the exciting story of Gideon, a farmer, won a war with Gods help. His weapons were a pitcher, a torch and a trumpet Judges chapters 6 and 7.

ROOSTER'S CROW

Deeply, Peter sunk into the blackness of despair.
He'd bragged about his courage, now he found it wasn't there.
He'd denied he even knew his Lord, as if he didn't care…
Now warmed himself before their fire. Such pain he could not bear.
And then the rooster crowed.

"Oh, Lord, forgive! I do not know what's coming over me!
I lied and turned my face around, not once, but times by three.
What now, Lord? I wait and weep. I pray on bended knee.
Lord, if You have mercy left, please, won't you hear my plea.
I heard my rooster crow.

"Lord, you always knew about me, that I'm only made of clay.
But with your Spirit, I will preach. You'll tell me what to say."
And He did!

Three thousand were converted, and they joined the church that day!
From the time the rooster crowed, Peter did not look away.
Thank you Lord for the rooster!

A rooster has a message.
It must sound the wake up call.
At times we seek to stand up strong, and only seem to fall.
We strive to be so big and brave, but all we feel is small.
It doesn't mean that life is gone. We're human, after all.
Listen for your rooster… flapping wings upon his wall….
It could be just your personal
wake up call!

..And Jesus said unto him, "Verily I say unto you, That this night, before the cock crow, thou shall deny me thrice." Matthew 26: 34

NOTE: The surrounding of the trial of Jesus, is described in the whole chapter 26.

JOSHUA SHOULDN'T'A DONE IT

It happened after Jericho fell,
God's word came down to Joshua
But he didn't listen well.

"As you conquer Canaan's land
You must make no peaceful treaty.
Just fight, and do what I command.

"If any nation is your friend
No treaty of peace should ever be made.
There'll be no quarrels for you to mend.

"I'm strong enough to fight your war.
When you make a pack, you're depending on another
You'll regret it, every more."

But no, he fell for Gibeon's lies
"These travelers came from such a long, long way
I must be very mighty in their eyes.

So, friends, we'll stand together, you and me.
No treaty with the enemy we will see."

...(Joshua said) Because you have beguiled us, saying "We are very far from you'... Joshua 9: 22

NOTE Because of the account of a treaty Joshua was instructed not to make, he found himself the protector of another country. He should not have made that treaty. Judges 9-11 gives the full account.

IF YOU BELIEVE...

If you believe…
  You will receive.

Old Daniel prayed…
  Inside his window every day.
He didn't care…
  Who heard the words he had to say.
His enemies…
  Told many hateful lies on him
And put him in…
  The lions den.

The king called out…
  But Dan said, "King, I'm still all right,
God took away…
  Their appetite!

If you believe…
  You will receive.

Three Hebrew boys…
  Refused to bow before the gold.
Why should they do…
  The evil they were sternly told?
The three were put…
  Into the fiery furnace flame
The king looked down…
  He saw what left him not the same.
"Did not we throw…
  Three in the fire? I see it's strangely odd
But one looks like…
  The Son of God.

If you believe…
  You will receive.

When Jonah heard…
  The scary words he heard God say,
He turned and took…
  A ship that went the other way.
A storm raged on…
  The sailors tossed him in the sea.
Then Jonah prayed…
  "I've messed up, God! Please, please save me!"
God made a fish…
  He was enormous… what a sight!
The big fish had…
  An appetite!

When Jonah prayed…
  His prayer was just a little late.
It took three days…
  For words to rise to heaven's gate.
The fish got sick…
  Of Jonah. (One can understand!)
It spit him out…
  Upon the land!

If you believe…
  You will receive.

Three thousand men…
  Surrounded Samson on the plain.
Though he was strong…
  They were determined he'd be slain.
He saw a bone…
  And then he knew he'd save his skin.
He swung and killed…
  A thousand men!

If you believe…
You will receive.
God will do just what
He said He'd do.
If you believe…
You will receive…
For every promise in the
Book belongs to you.

"And all things, whatsoever ye ask in prayer, believing, ye shall receive." Matthew 21:22

NOTE: This is a lighthearted exhortation on faith.

SILVER DAGGER

Use what you have….

It was made of silver.
Born in furnace fire
It drew a cooling breath, deep cradled in its form.
Dug from the mountain
Cloaked in mud,
A special ore, possessing strength above the norm.
And beauty deep within…
A shining spire!
It has a lofty purpose… This dagger must perform
A task truly enormous!
Frightening… dire!
Please, God! Success! Else a sheer, political storm!
This instrument of evil
Will have no buyer!

Israel, again, was captured.
Eighteen long years.
Much too long. Since back when Ehud was a laughing child.
But now no laughter.
Only flowing tears.
This weapon was an answer. Carefully… it was styled.
Solid hasp to grip,
Where blade adheres.
Fat King Eglon. While he rules, God's Israel is defiled.
Please, God, success!
See bitter tears?
The young man wrapped an empty gift… and smiled.
The dragon on the handle!
Creating fears!

In his summer house
King was at rest.

Laid back! Proud! Was he not the king of all the land?
Footsteps soft, breath silent.
Ehud faces test.
Use what he had. It was a great skill in his left hand.
The gift in right hand
Held at his chest.
Dagger in the skillful left hand, controlled command.
Hid in his garment
There below his vest!

Gift from a stranger?
Welcome guest!
Fat King smiled. He never knew he'd soon be dead.
So, look more friendly.
A smiling face.
Ehud moved toward the king, still lounging in his bed.
The empty gift extended,
Left hand in place.
He came in range… a cleansing breath to clear his head.
Greedy King reached for the gift,
Ehud, thrust in haste…
Into the rounded belly. Through the fat… a flow of red.
Fat King expected praises.
But got a taste.
Of young man's anger. Dagger entered fatness… instead.
Fat swallowed up the dagger.
Worthwhile waste!

Ehud did his homework.
No skill was thought too small.
Weapons at the ready. Wait for results of Ehud's charm.
Men came from the mountains
At Ehud's trumpet call.
Trumpets, spears and daggers, clutched in each strong, young arm.
King's soldiers shot their dice
In barracks hall.
While King bled in summer house, Ehud's anger brought their harm.
They spread about like honey
Silent army… all.

Enemy surrounded. No King to muster soldiers. No general's alarm.
Slaughter, far and wide!
See armed soldiers fall!
Finally came the word! The King! The King! Alas, too late!
His left hand had a value… Repeat…
No skill is ever small!

God has ways to bridge the difference
Between man's ability
And the job He must have done. A bit of anger has its uses.
Greedy King distracted.
All he could see
Was a gift that he did not deserve. Forgot all the abuses
In eighteen years of reign.
Such agony!
But Ehud's strong LEFT arm still sustained him

NO EXCLUSES

…And Ehud put forth his left hand and took the dagger from his right thigh, and thrust it into (the King's) belly, and the haft also went in after the blade, and the fat closed upon the blade so that he could not draw the dagger out…..

NOTE: This account of the left handed dagger maker and the way he won a war is detailed in Judges 3: 16-30

HAMMER IN HAND

Jael had always lived in tents.
It only made a lot of sense
If she would be with Heber on the battle field…indeed!
For Heber fought with saber… bright!
He charged out bravely, what a sight!
The hammer and the tent spikes were all Jael would need.

On her knees before the fire
She fed the sticks, and flames went higher.
She pounded grain and made her flour as fine as battle dust.
Tent walls of skin enclosed her life,
For Jael was a soldier's wife,
She knew her place in life and she would do the things she must.

While all around the battle raged
And Israel's bravest men engaged.
But Sisera and his evil troops advanced with victory shout.
Should Israel fight… or run away?
And live to fight another day?
Barak, the general of the troops had much to think about.

Deborah, prophetess, sought God's word
And this is what the general heard,
"Go to, fight on, and final victory will be given you."
Siscera's army raged about
And Barak entertained a doubt.
"I'll go and fight if only you will come on, too."

Deborah told him, "I will go
But here's one thing you have to know,
You'll win, but it will be a woman who'll receive the glory."
Barak, with Deborah by his side
An armored steed he chose to ride.
He'd fight, and did not care if victory was a woman's story.

Jael crouched upon the sand,
The hammer stone within her hand.
She sought to pound the grain she'd use to cook the evening meal.
A mighty war horse, man astride,
Then Siscera stood there by her side
With his armor-sagging shoulders, and a wan and weary feel.

Then she went pale with awful fright,
His sword could kill! It was his right!
She was his foe. A thrust of sword could quickly run her through!
Quick! Think! Could she pretend…
That she saw him only as a friend?
She must decide which way was right. What was the best thing she could do?

With her hammer stone in hand,
Her agile mind took full command!
"Come in, my lord, and rest, while I make you a goodly meal."
Milk and meat would be his wish
And precious butter from a dish,
Then she spread the bed, inviting him to take a nap to heal.

And when his eyes were closed in sleep,
On silent knees she sought to creep
To where her extra tent spikes lay. They made a tidy, shiny pile.
Her trembling hand picked up the best
And sharpest…pounding heart within her chest,
She crawled back to the sleeping man. Fear shook her all the while.

Her hammer stone lay on the sand,
Pointed tent spike in her hand
She poised the shiny point above the weary, sleeping head.
The stake, now steady in her hand,
She made the hammer stone to land.
A deadly blow. She nailed him to the rocky ground, and he was dead.

Then Jael had no time to loose
But ran to Heber with the news.
And Barak knew that Siscera was now dead. The battle had been won.
The women in the tents all know

What Jael's bravery had to show.
They sang the songs of praise describing all deeds that she'd done.

"Into the tent she led him,
With butter she had fed him,
She covered him and let him rest his body on the ground.
With tent spike and a hammer, too,
Her willing hand knew what to do.
She pounded and she nailed him to the earth with just one mighty pound!

"The wife of Heber," soldiers said,
"Slew mighty Siscera on his bed!"
The fighting men came safely home and gladly told the story.
Just as Deborah told Barak,
It was with a woman's act
The war was won by her, and she would now receive the glory.

A thousand years have past and gone.
But some brave deeds live on and on.
The world can read the story how the women sang their song.
And history sings of Jael's praise,
How on that special day of days,
There was a cowardly man…
And finally glory went where glory should belong!

…Then Jael, Heber's wife, took a nail of the tent, and took an hammer in her hand and went softly unto him and smote the nail into his temples and fastened it into the ground, for he was fast asleep and weary. So he died. Judges 4: 21

NOTE: Through an act of deception, the woman killed an enemy king by nailing his head to the floor of her tent. The women of Israel sang a song to her bravery. The whole account is in Judges 4 and 5.

BAD LUCK! NO TONGUE!

A man took a sail on Galilee
Because his boat was new.
He dropped a gold coin overboard.
No problem. He had quite a few.

Over, under, flashed the coin
Above a greedy fish.
Flipped and whirled in bright sunlight
It slowly fell, a wavy wallow.
The coin fit in the fish's mouth
Or almost… Just about!
But fishes have no 'huff' or 'puff',
He couldn't even spit it out.

When it was time for taxes
Peter wondered what to do.
Jesus said, "Go net a fish.
When a fish flops in the net,
Go pay the tax for me and you
With the coin that wouldn't fit."
The reason Peter caught that fish,
Is… that fishes just can't spit.

Perhaps the coin was just enough
For taxes he must pay.
I think the fish was so relieved,
He flipped his tail and swam away.

….Notwithstanding, lest we should offend them, go thou to the sea, and cast an hook, and take up the fish that first cometh up, and when your hast opened his mouth, thou shalt find a piece of money. Take that, and give it to them for me and thee. Matthew 17:24

NOTE: this is a light-hearted parody surrounding the payment of taxes that Jesus did not owe. The Pharisees were trying to trap Jesus. Matthew 17: 24-27

STIR UP THE NEST

The eagle's nest was lined with grass
  And feathers, soft as thistledown.
With eggs, softly then protected,
  Thirty feet from off the ground.

Twigs and thorns and vines were used
  To build the eagle's deep nest bowl.
But, only softness for the chicks
  Lined within the entire whole.

As time went on, the fluff was crushed
  As chicks were near to fledge.
The parents took great beaks of it
  And tossed it from the edge.

Thorn spikes that had been hidden
Now poked into the nest.
Chicks lying down for comfort, now,
Had no place where they could rest.

So…

On the nest rim stood the chicks
  Flapped their wings and squealed with rage,
And rose into the air and flew…
  … The parents said,
"Another brood has come of age!"

"… I put thee in remembrance that thou stir up the gift of God, which in in thee…" II Timothy 1:6

NOTE: The Apostle, Paul, reminded young Timothy that he must use the gift of the "faith that is in thee, which dwelt first in thy grandmother, Lois, and thy mother, Eunice". Young Timothy was becoming too comfortable.

Occasionally, God must make life uncomfoftable, to get humans to pay attention.

(From Grandpa's Sermon)

PARABLE OF THE TREES.

The trees all decided a wonderful thing. They'd all get together and vote in a king.
They need a ruler to keep them all in line. Among them, the olive, the fig tree and vine.

They sought for a
Candidate, mainly
in vain. The mere
thought of running
gave good trees
A pain.

Then one accepted.
An offer was made.
The bramble said,
"Sure! You can
dwell in my shade."

Before it was over,
No one had a doubt.
They'd be much better
off if they'd gone
on without.

God needed a
messenger, asked,
"Who will it be?"
Isiah replied, "Lord,
I'm here. Just
send me."

The answer is simple. In fact, nothing to it.
So much can done, by those willing to do it.

One of the saddest things under the sun… is a person of worth who refuses to run.
That leaves the job open for trash and debris. "Lord… I'm here. Just send me!"

This is an interesting parable about the politics of choosing a leader and ending up with the worst possible candidate after being turned down by better ones. Judges 9: 8-16

MAGNIFICENT FOOTSTEPS

Sore feet. Bandaged. Raw and Sore. A starving man released a sigh. Drew in his ragged cloak and uttered "Why sit we here until we die? There is no food within the city, at least, there is no food for us. So, why would we expend the effort? It would use up energy to fuss."

Samaria, once a tall proud fortress
Now hid behind its walls and cried.
Their hated enemy besieged their city,
Many from within had died.

OUTSIDE THE WALLS

"So here we sit, outcast and hungry.
Leperous sores from head to feet.
We know no food is ever coming.
The city has no food to eat.

"So why are we still out here sitting?
Waiting till we lie down dead.
Marauder's tents are not far from us…
Why not go that way, instead?"

The four men looked at one another.
There seemed to be no more to say.
So what if they met swords and arrows?
Sitting, they'd soon die, anyway!"

One sore foot before the other,
Softly on the ground they tread.
Perhaps they would be met with mercy,
Perchance there'd be a bite of bread.

Of course, it could have been God's timing.
Footsteps placed with awful dread.
God magnified pathetic footsteps,
To be an army's march, instead.

Footsteps. Painful. Slowly forward
Sound like drumbeat in the tent.
Dry earth shook with loud vibrations.
Sounding like a regiment.

THE ENEMY

Leaving food and fire and clothing,
Frightened.. trembling, pale with fright.
Away they ran across the desert,
Soon were fully out of sight.

THE LEPERS

Footsteps stepping through the tent door not knowing if they soon would die. What they saw within the tent door was amazing to their eye! Clothing, weapons, swords!
Everything they saw looked good. But, best of all, they saw a cook fire. Above the fire was good, warm food.

They ate and ate,

and finally had their fill

And then they had a

thought of pity.

They should take

news to the hungry

Crouched behind

walls… in the city.

MAGNIFICANCE

Now, there are
more words one could say,
When those sore
feet touched the ground,
The faintest
whisper of their footsteps
Became a
frightening, thunderous sound.

In truth, the soldiers
in the tent homes
Thought that
somehow in the night
An army came wit
strength and weapons.
And they were here,
prepared to fight.

If God could
magnify the footsteps
Of a starving,
hurting man, just think
What God can do if
one is willing…
And will do the best
he can?

Oh yes! There's
much more to be telling
Before and after this
event.
About what
happened in the city
When they heard

about the tent.

Sometimes lessons
hide in stories
Or just a word
within a rhyme.
All God needs are
willing footsteps,
To show his Power
every time!

"…the Lord had made the host of Syrians to hear a nose of chariots and a noise of horses, even the nose of a great host…"

NOTE: a marvelous account of four lepers whose weak feet were made to sound like an army, and the enemy was frightened away. The whole 7th chapter furnishes interesting details.

LAMP UNTO MY FEET

I'd love to hold light overhead,

To see my footsteps as I tread

This rocky pathway where I'm led.

The reason is, I've often said,

If I saw obstacles ahead

I'd choose another path, instead.

But...........................

Light at my feet, it has to stay

So step by step and day by day,

I pray my steps will never stray.

So, though I would my fears allay,

And hurry on without delay...

I will need patience, Lord I pray,

To use the Light... shone on my way.

"...Thy word is a lamp unto my feet and a light unto my path." Psa 119:105

NOTE: The light moves ahead only as fast as the feet can walk

CAREFUL... WHERE YOU PUT YOUR ' BUT'.

I would love to tell you more
BUT it would only make you sore.

I really like your new hairdo,
BUT I think the gray should be less blue.

Your vacation shots are nice
BUT I've already seen them twice.

I'd love to come and help you move
BUT I just can get in the groove.

I'm really sorry to be rude
BUT I'm in a lousy, awful mood.

A piece of truth, and so clear cut…
It matters where you put your 'but'.
One word is tricky, and what's more,
It cancels out what's said before.

"…But let your communication be, Yea,Yea (or) Nay Nay, for whatsoever is more than these cometh of evil." Matthew 5:37

VENGENCE ISN'T OURS

"Vengence is Mine!"
God spoke those words just like he meant them.
"I will repay!"
Other efforts mean we will repent them.

The King Solomon
Suggested another way. A way we might allay our wrath.
There was a way…
The scene could be accomplished by another path.

If it should be,
Your enemy is hungry, you must feed him well.
If he is thirsty
Give him drink, and that is really all there is to tell.

By doing that
"Coals of fire would be piled on his head!"
And all it costs
Is just a bit of water, and a generous piece of bread.

The water is,
A total attitude of such forgetfulness
No one could tell
That what had happened caused us much distress.

The food could be:
A kindness shown in such a quiet, loving way
With no confrontation.
A smile and kindly word would be a gift meant to defray.

The wise would say,
That wise old Solomon, in Proverbs, also said
That it would heap
Hot coals of fire there upon his head!

And it could be
You'd have a friend. The former enemy was dead.
But all I know
Is what I read of words the wise king said!

"…And unto him that smiteth thee on one cheek offer also the other, and let him that taketh away they cloke forbid not to take they cloak also." Luke 6: 29

THIRSTY CAMELS AT THE WELL

(foretelling the dispute between Jews and Arabs)

There is another tale to tell
As camels stood beside the well
They were just about a thirsty as a came could get, but yet…
The man was thirsty, too
But he had a job to do.
He had a question he must ask. What kind of answer would he get?

He'd come fro far away
A journey of more than a day.
He came to get a bride for his good master, Abraham's, son
How would he know which one
Would be best for the son,
So he asked God to help him out, so he could pick the one

The question:
"Would you ever be so kind,
Are you sure you woundn't mind
Could I drink from your pitcher? My journey has been long?"
He'd make a deal with God
And sealed it with a nod.
If this girl offered water for the camels, she would be the one.

The girl. Che didn't ba a eye,
Or let a moment pass her by.
With water pitcher she stood right there by the well.
And said, "Sir, you may have a drink.
Another thing I also think,
That I should also draw up water fill your camels get their fill."

This was how the servant knew
His strange search was now through.
He gave the girl the presents that his master sent for her.
She said that on that very day,

She was ready to go away.
If fact, she would start right now if he would prefer.
That's how Isaac met his wife
To make his happy all his life.
She bore a pair of twin boys who gave her quite a pain.
They fought before the two were born.
God had words for her to warn,
Her two sons would become two nations, that was plain.

The nations could not get along.
Both had warrior big and strong.
And for years and centuries it would always be that way.
Their disagreements mounted.
Casualties were un counted.

They would be enemies, and that would last till judgment day.

…And she made haste and let down her pitcher from her shoulder and said, "Drink, and I will give they camels drink also…Genesis 24:46

NOTE: complete details are found in Genesis chapter 24.

5+2= PLENTY
(with 12 remainder)

Jesus spoke, there was so much to say.
The hungry crowd, 5,000 strong, will waited
Stores for food were many miles away.

Concerned disciples came to say,
"Master these are weak from huger.
Please send them on their way."

Jesus said, "So we will give them food."
"But, Master, they are very hungry.
We have no answer that id good

Jesus said, "What do we have?"
"Nothing, Master. All we have is just
A tiny, little lunch a small boy gave."

"Bring it," said Jesus. And he turned aside.
He blessed the lunch, the loaves of five
And fishes, too. The food then multiplied.

The disciples served the hungry crowd,
And they all were filled with food.
The disciple's all were very proud.

It seemed the best food every tasted.,
But scraps must all be gathered
So nothing would ever be wasted.

The disciples gathered fish and bread.
Twelve baskets were filled up.
So that is why it could be said,

"That five plus two does not make seven,
(with twelve baskets still left over!)"
If it's been blessed by One from heaven?

Could it be possible that
Human numbers do
Not matter all
That much
To..
God?

… And they did all eat, and were filled: and they took kup of the fragments that remained twelve baskets full.

And they that had eaten were about five thousand men, beside women and children… Matthew 14:20- 21

Note: Background incidents are in Chapter 14 of Genesis.

THE SICK FISH

When God said, "Jonah, you must go,
Then Jonah promptly answered "No,"
"I'll not go to Nineveh. Those people are just too bad," he said."
And old Jonah on that very day
Thought he would go another way.
He bought a ticket, came aboard the ship and promptly went to bed.

God was so very angry he
Sent down a wild and stormy sea.
The frightened sailors, did their best and then began to pray.
Each one prayed to his own god
Of course, their prayers were never heard.
They finally woke up Jonah to help them pray the storm away.

But Jonah said he could not pray,
That he had tried to disobey,
And now his God was angry, so he must be thrown out overboard.
They did not wish him to die,
But now they knew the reason why.
He said to pitch him in the sea, and they took him at his word.

God was ready with a hungry fish.
If to disobey was Jonah's wish
A little while within the fish, would give him time for thinking
The fierce wild winds and stormy sea
Became calm as a cup of tea,
And the happy sailors in the boat had no more fear of sinking.

So Jonah spent…

Three days and nights upon his knees
Within the fish… no moment's ease,
Until he prayed and told God that he would gladly now obey.
He'd go to Nineveh and say

That God on the fortieth day
Would destroy the city, and that's exactly what he would say.

God gave the fish a belly ache.
Jonah had a trip to make.
The fish swam to the shore and spit him out upon dry land.
So Jonah went to Nineveh then
And preached to them about their sin.
And they repented, prayed, and hoped Jonah's God would understand.

Jonah preached but he was mad.
His actions made his God quite sad,
To have his folks refuse to go to where he wished for them to go.
 It would be easy at this time to think that the fish
  Was not really very happy, either.

..."The Lord spake unto the fish, and it vomited out Jonah on dry land." Jonah, 2: 10

NOTE: For the whole account of Jonah's difficulty in obeying God, the whole book of Jonah (containing 4 chapters), gives the details.

UNLUCKY THIRTEEN

Should old thirteen deserve the shame
 To have 'unlucky' as its name?
What did it ever do to deserve that?   What was so bad?
For back in history one could go,
 Back to the town of Jericho
Thick walls of stone and mortar were the thing that city had.

God said, "I'll give to you the town,
 And all the walls will crumble down
And never will there be a weapon in any warrior's hand."
God's people crossed the Jordan's tide
 While feet of priests just stood aside,
And let the people pass them by to enter the new land.

The people marched one time each day
 Until six days had gone away
And on the seventh day they marched it seven times around.
Then the people halted steps…
 The priests put trumpets to their lips.
All creatures in the desert heard the dreadful trumpet sound.

Shouts and cries of people calling,
 Grinding rocks and mortar falling
Till strong thick walls of Jericho were absolutely gone!
 (All except Rahab's apartment.)
It would seem that six times and seven
 Were a mandate down from heaven,
One's luck depends, most likely, on Whose side that one was on.
 (The marching army outside the walls
 seemed extremely lucky!)

MORE THIRTEENS… JUST A COINCIDENCE?

There were 13 tribes of Israel (Joseph's tribe was divided to his sons.)
There were 13 Federated colonies in America. The dollar bill
Has 13 stars over the eagle
And 13 letters in the motto over its head.
There are 13 paleways in the eagle's shield. The right talon has olive
Branches with 13 olive leaves, and
13 olive fruits. The left talon
Has 13 arrows fletched with
13 feathers. They pyramid
Has 13 courses of masonry. The United States flag has
13 stripes.

...And ye shall compass the city...and go around the city once. Thus shalt thou do six days. ...and the seventh day ye shall compass the city seven times, and the priests shall blow with the trumpets.

...and when ye hear the sound of the trumpet, all the people shall shout with a great shout, and the wall of the city shall fall down flat... Joshua 6: 3-5

THEY HAD A MIND TO WORK

The walls of great Jerusalem had tumbled down with years.
When Nehemiah heard it, it almost gave him tears.

So Nehemiah led his band. To the city he woud go.
He could build that wall again, for God had told him so.

Sanballot lived outside the wasl. He liked it in array.
He said, "What do these feeble Jews? Repair it in a day?"

"Will they remove this pile of stones ? Are they bound?
His friend, Tobiah, said
A fox could easily break it down."

But Nehemiah did not stop. The wall began to grow.
The people had a mind to work, and it would not be slow.

Sanballot shot his arrow, in an attack against the wall.
Nehemiah armed the workers, the arrows came right back!

The builders toiled and work so hard, the wall began to climb.
They would soon the town enclose, if they just had the time.

When it came time to build the gates, he took men with great skill.
These skilled men brought sons along, and they worked with a will.

But Shallum had no sons to bring, but that did not make him wait.
He brought along his daughters and they helped him build his gate.

They worked in blowing wind. They worked in rain and sun.
God put strength within they hands and worked till work was done.

Young and old and large and small. There was no place to lurk.
The wall grew higher every day and no one tried to shirk,

Nehemiah said it was because
"The people had a mind to work."

...And they said, "Let us rise up and build" So they strengthen their hands for this good work. Nehemiah 2:18

...So built we the wall: and all the wall was joined together unto the half thereof, for the people had a mind to work... Nehemiah 6:6

NOTE: Details of the wall-building are found in the book of Nehemiah.

THE DAY THE SUN STOOD STILL

Joshua chased the enemy over forest, plain and field
Five kings challenged him to war, and Joshua would not yield.

He chased them to a valley, and there they chose to fight.
They turned and fought until the day was almost become night.

Joshua's army struggled on. The sun was getting loser.
Sometimes the fighting speeded up and other times got slower.

Sometimes it seemed that he would win, and then he seemed to lose.
It was the time for choices. Which way would he choose?"

If the sun went down right now, they couldn't see to fight.
The enemy would bring new soldiers by in the dark of night.

When the morning sun came up, reinforcements would be there.
While Joshua's tired army was the same. It would not be fair.

It wasn't looking very good if he ran out of day.
He couldn't give the enemy a chance to run away.

Joshua bravely raised his eyes to One who made the sun.
If anyone could stop it, that God would be that one.

Joshua looked up to the sky. "Sun, stand thou still!" he said.
Than that old sun did not go down. Stayed where it was instead.

The way the enemy had to fight. The five kings ran away.
In a cave they hid themselves, and they stayed there all day.

Joshua's army won the war, and Joshua went to see
The five kings had to die, and Joshua hung them from a tree.

The God who heard when Joshua called, still rules the sky today.

...Then spake Joshua to the Lord in the day when the Lord delivered up the Amorites before the children of Israel, and he said in the sight of Israel. "Sun, stand thou still upon Gibeon, and thou, Moon, in the valley of Ajalon."

And the sun stood still, and the moon stayed until the people had avenged themselves upon their enemies... Joshua 10: 12-13

NOTE: Chapter 10 contains details of this battle, and of the killing of the 5 kings in verse 22

VAPOR AND FLAME

(Written from the viewpoint of a young soldier, when Israel's cowards refused to conquer Jericho, and they must wait until everyone over 40 died in the wilderness.)

So temporary.
So much now on the move.
Nothing solid to hand onto, and now we follow a cloud and a flame.

After the failure at Jericho, the fire and cloud turned right.
The cloud we see above us… moving slowly. Fire at night.
We came of Jericho, now we're leaving, because of fright.

There we were all camping in our tents on desert sand.
A discontented crowd of humans. A tawdry, hungry band.
Life in tents, sand underfoot. Nothing we could understand.

We still had the cloud by day and pillar of fire by night.
We were being lead away. We must keep our guide in sight.
Until they died, there in the wilderness. Aimless as a kite.

Of course, it is the only thing we young folks knew
For all our lives, the babes were born, and children grew
Living on the manna that came each morning like the dew.

THey wander here and there, and waited for forty years to die.
All of those who were afraid, and had no courage just to try
To conquer Jericho. They preferred to let the chance go by.

But time passed

Then we were back on Jordan's bank, where our brave stood
And faced the giants in the land, as we always knew they should.
We will possess the land, because God said we would.

The guiding cloud of vapor, no longer needed, slipped away.
There was no need for a fiery pillar to protect us from the fray.
We stood on the doorstep of our new home. a brand new day.

Ahead was Jericho, it's walls were high and very, very wide.
We didn't try to fight or gain a way to get inside.
We only marched, our feet kept time, we did not try to hide.

Thirteen times we circled 'round and round that wicked wall.
We marched while laughter from inside would taunt us all,
But we all kept marching, tall and short, large and small.

Thirteen times, and the wll came down! What a sight!
It fell, and not because of any skills or any might.
It fell by faith in God, and no one actually had to fight.
We conquered Jericho. For us it was a sheer delight!

All it took was bravery…

And God!

"…And it shall come to pass, that when (the priests) make a long blast with the ran's horn and when ye hear the sound of the trumpet, all the people shall shout with a great shout, and the wall of the city shall fall down flat,,, Joshua 6:5

NOTE: For a complete picture of the fall of Jericho, see chapeters 5 and 6 of the book of Joshua.

TWO TRIPS TO SEE THE POTTER

It took two trips. Two trips… one trip would not have been enough.
I had much to tell my people. There were important lessons all
should hear.
It had to take two trips, as lessons, to see the potter at his work,
For such important lessons what I'm saying, should very, crystal clear.
The potters house was nearby, handy, the place of lessons closely by.
Where daily scoops of softened clay were put upon the turning wheel.
It was the business of the potter. Pots were to be made…tall jars for
the wine.
Sharp tools would decorate the vessels. Designs would add to their
appeal.

The first thing, foremost of all other, the clay must be made smooth.
With the turning of the wheel, the sides are thin and tight.
Strong fingers of the potter work to shape the walls and neck,
As the potter's wheel is turning, hands build in the strength and
height.
Like soft breezes, potter's skillful fingers flow across the satin clay.
Smoothing out the tucks and creases, dips and small, uneven bumps.
One thing the potter must remember … in any vessel ever made
He must be sure, there'll never be, no, never ever! any lumps.

The vessel sets, no drop of moisture, and not a substance, foreign,
The sculpted vessel, dry and stiffened must be ready for the fire.
The work is done. There'll be no changes. What is made, is made.
The roar of flames will assault the eardrums, ever hot and higher
Gentle care while in the turning, now careful carving had been done.
The fully sculpted, finished vessel sets within the flaming pyre.
The gradual heat at first, begins to warm the clay. Refinish must be
slow.
The mud is now no longer mud, changes made within the fire.

BUT…

If a lump of unmixed product is allowed to remain within the jar
Set in the unforgiving furnace heat, no allowance for mistake.
The jar reacts to rising heat waves… the lump within the jar will not.
At some point the lump explodes, and that is when the jar will break!

SO…

When the softened clay is riding of the potters turning wheel,
It is crushed and pressed and kneaded, back into its heap of mud.
Now the foreign lump is taken, tossed away. New vessel formed.
It was not the potter's first choice. Not as tall, but still it's good.

JEREMIAH WATCHED.

The lump came out, the wheel began to turn, the pot was then remade.
The potter's mind had seen the vessel, fingers all had shaped the line.
A lighter touch is needed here, and then a firmer pressure there
It took the cutting of the sculpture knife to create the design.
It's now a smaller jar. The lump is gone… and with it, size.
Not his first choice, but as he studied it, he saw it pleased the eye.
His mind still saw the finished jar, his fingers knew the shape
It was a pleasing vessel. He nodded, noting, with a sigh.

LESSON FINISHED

Then God told Jeremiah, "Look and see.
You've seen the future of the House of Israel.
Write for me the things your eye has seen.
You're to tell my children. See you write it well."

Jeremiah's pen then wrote this in his book
"House of Israel, you must never fear.
I promise you'll become my people,
And when you seek me, I'll be ever near.

"You'll be walking through the nations
And as you go, your strength will gain.
You'll fall before the world's diseases
But you will learn to live with pain.
Then, I'll sift you through the nations
I must remove your lump of sin.
Yet all the time my eye is still upon you,
And nothing will have ever been in vain..
I'll make you sleep through many ages,
You will not know where you've been.
Through the heathen I will drive you
Removing filthiness… sin… debris,
So, when at last you come to Zion
I will be pleased. You will be free.

Everything I've have scattered, I will gather
Everything I've have bound, I will set loose.
I'll press you, crush you, and remake you.
But what I have destroyed, I'll reproduce.
Though I said one time, 'You're not my people',
I promise you will all be Mine again.
And all the time My eye is there upon you.
Nothing, I have done, will be in vain."

Recall the words I said of my son, Isaac,
"In Isaac will my name be called," because
Abraham, my friend, was ever with me,
He loved me, and he always loved my laws.
Isaac's sons will conquer many nations,
Isaac's sons will tame the rolling seas.
'Sax Sons are the ones to tell My Greatness
Saxons will be the ones who try to please.
I led Saxons safely through the nations,
I helped them as they fled captivity.

Through the rugged mountains of Caucasia
I led you through the cruel mountain pass.
All the world will know it is Caucasians,
My servants, helpers, they'll become at last.

...

...

THEN

Jeremiah, at the potters, watching at the turning wheel once more
This time he took a vessel, finished, hardened by the fire.
He took it to the ancients of the people, and of the priests.

Before the eyes of priests and men, inside the eastern gate. it shattered.
The pieces lay in dusty piles of rubble at their feet upon the ground.
Tiny pieces hid in grass roots, while the clay dust floated on the wind.
All the broken parts that made the bottle, never would again be found.

GOD SAID

This bottle, broken, is the House of Judah
You see it cannot ever be redeemed.
In time, it will be crushed in many pieces
And never will it be complete again.

Then you'll see the kingly line of Judah
Will be found within the House of Israel.
David's Greater Son will rule my people
As you have heard My promise to you tell.
I've said that I will always have a people.
I've promised I will guide them to My land.
Even when they think they do not know Me
I will hold them safely in My hand.

The day will come to see House of Judah
Peaceful when it's joined with Israel
My Hand will lead them safely to New Zion
And there, forever, they will safely dwell.
Again they'll plant their seed and reap a harvest
Grow olives trees, and grain to make their bread.
I've promised I will always have a people.
You must tell my people what I've said.

SO JEREMIAH WROTE.

Time, and times again, words written on the pages of my book
The House of Israel, is driven. And I will sift them, everyone.
The House of Israel have I scattered… closed their eyes in sleep.
I will gather what I've scattered when their punishment is done.
I have always kept my promise, what I've said, I'll surely do.
Memories of their wandering, here I promise, will be none.

Those asleep will then awaken, eyes will know me, knees will bow.
Remnant of the House of Israel, and any left in Judah, will be one.
But this I say, it's only for My glory. I must do this in the heathen's eyes.
So they will see this is My doings, that what I've said that I will do….

Now is done!

This is the saga built around the prophesy concerning Israel and Judah, based on Jeremiah chapters 18 and 19

BLESSED STABLE AT THE INN

Joseph, footsoe, weary, put one foot before the other to lead the donkey on the rocky road. Mary,, anxious, in discomfort rode. So soon to be a mother.

The journey down from Nazareth at Herod's stern decree was a necessary pause within their lives. To all be counted, to be taxed and to pay the legal fee.

Bethlehem, a tiny town, now holds its multitudes. All members of the house of David came. Provisions for the travelers were, at once, inadequate and crude.

The inns in Bethlemem were quickly filling up to burst. Still they came, the road was crowded still with travelers, hoping there was food and drink, so weary of their thirst.

The long rooms in the inn were filled with pallets, end to end. Families crowded closely, hardy room for comfort. Weary children, tiredly fussy, arguments erupt, loud voices to contend.

When the inn was full and not one more could be squeezed, the keeper turned his mind to rent the outer yard. A space of ground. The traveler who could get it would be pleased.

By nightfall every courtyard space was filled to overflowing. They found safety from the robbers on the streets. The crowds around the city walls and streets were quickly growing.

Then, through the city gates, the donkey plodded swaying 'neath the load. And Mary rode, her body aching sore from labor pains. Joseph, brow furred with concern, eyes down cast upon the rocky road.

He worked his tired steps one at a time between the crowds along the street, dismayed and heavy hearted that he had arrived so very late.

He inn was full, the courtyard was full. It hardly left a place to plant his feet.

The harried keeper of the inn told Joseph sad words that he already knew. He also saw the cause of Joseph's plight. What could be done? Poor wife! Surely there was something … Oh, yes, there was a thing that he could do.

"Sir, there is one place to stay…I've saved it… for it my animal' stable cave. Your wife could rest. You could feed your donkey on the straw. I know your wife is in great need, and I have held it special. My friend, it's all I have."

Joseph's frowning brow smoothed, and his pounding heart was finally stilled. At last there was a place! For Mary's time was now! There was a place, the babe would come, and prophesy would be fulfilled.

No crowded, noisy, smelly room with strangers to the left and right. No listening to their neighbor's tales of woe nearby. No travelers looking on, for this was surely Mary's night.

Night darkness closed protectively around the humble stable cave. Inside? The Son of God came down to earth! God, smiling on His son, gave to him the best that Heaven had!

The stable cave was softly quiet. The ox and donkey breathed relaxing sighs. They quietly stood there chewing on the manger straw. Thick walls shielded from the chill of night and from the prying human eyes.

The sky above the shepherds on the hillside close behind the town burst forth with angel wings and joyous songs! The shepherds did as they were told. Excited footsteps brought them down to town.

The angels told the shepherds and the shepherds told each other all the wonders that had happened in the stable by the inn. They gazed in wonder at the Baby, in the arms of His young mother.

Heavenly Father, in His caring way had held… for them… the stable. Warm and private, for the birthing of his Son.

So stand amazed, ye humans of the earth!
Your God is great and He is able!

...And brought forth her first born son and wrapped him in swaddling clothes, and laid him in a manger, because there was no room for them in the inn... Luke 2:7

NOTE: The entire second chapter tells the Christmas story.

THE DAY THE ROCKS AND WATER BURNED

The day that rocks and water burned,
Was made a lesson to be learned.

Elijah stood on Carmel's Mount
While all Baal's prophets stood about.

"This is the day," Elijah cried
"This a test. Baal will be tried.

"We need two alters, side by side,
And on each one a bull is tied.

"We'll worship God. No other name!
We'll call our Gods. Each by his name.

"Just tell your God to send the fire!
Speak up loud! And cry out, higher!

"Perhaps this is Baal's visiting day,
"Or he's asleep, or gone away!"

Elijah taunted, as they prayed,
And cut with knives, and with whips flayed.

No fire came down. The day was 'ore.
Baal prophets bled, their voices sore.

And then Elijah took a turn.
There was a lesson yet to learn.

Twelve stones had built the alter high
And still no fire came from the sky.

Twelve barrels of water, poured around.
It soaked the bull, the rocks and ground.

He put a trench around the stones
 The bull was soaked, down to the bones.

Elijah stood, they heard him say.
 "Lord, let them know this very day.

"That Israel's God told words to me.
 This very day the world will see,

"Your power come down in flames of fire,
 And let the heat of flames go higher.

"To burn the offering and the stones,
 And burn the sticks and burn the bones."

"Show to those prophets as they scoff,
 "That fire burns water in the trough."

The fire came down, the flames grew higher.
 It burned the bull and stones with fire.

The fire the water could not quench
 Licked up the water in the trench.

That day a lesson clear was learned,
 When bull, and rocks, and water burned!
  And God gave Baal just what he'd earned!

"...Then the fire of the Lord fell, and consumed the burnt sacrifice, and the wood, and the stones, and the dust and licked up the water that was in the trench. And when all the people saw it, they fell on their faces: and they said, The Lord, he is the God, the Lord, he is the God." Kings 18:38-39

NOTE: The whole exciting account of the sacrifices and the miracle are detailed in I Kings Chapter 18.

THE LITTLE BOAT, TWICE OWNED

Small Tommy, with his tacks and wood,
Made a boat, and thought it good.
With a brush and can of paint,
He made it look the way it should.

But when he took it out to play
The errant boat swam far away
Following after other toys
Belonging to some other boys.

Tommy was forlorn and sad
He missed his boat, the one he had.
In a junk shop window he could see,
There was his boat! Sure as could be!

Dirty, paint-chipped, ragged sail.
The price of it was one whole dime.
Tommy ran home for his money
And he got back just in time.

He cleaned the dirt, repaired the sail
And painted. What a sight to see!
Smiling, Tommy told the toy,
"Now, two times, you belong to me.

"I made you and I lost you…
I found you, and I paid my dime.
I bought you and I loved you.
I saw through all your grime.

"I cleaned you and I painted you,
Now you're a thing to see.
I made you and I bought you,
Now you twice belong to me!"

"…ye are not your own, for ye are bought with a price…" I Corinthians 6: 20-21

NOTE: This the perfect illustration of how God created humans, they willingly strayed and he bought they back again by his death on the cross. Therefore, humans following him are 'twice owned.'
(from Grandpa's sermon)

THE LITTLE MOUSE

Once a trap was baited with a tiny piece of cheese.
It tickled so a little mouse, it almost made him sneeze!

The old mouse said, "Be careful! There's danger if you go."
The little mouse said "Phooy! I don't think you know.

He watched that little piece of cheese and couldn't look away.
He thought about that cheese so much, he couldn't even play.

He came a little closer and he got a better sight…
It smelled so good, he even thought he'd take a little bite.

The old mouse said, "Forget that cheese and hurry out to play"
But cheese smelled so delicious he just couldn't walk away.

""I only want to taste it. Would that not be all right?"
So first he took a nibble and then he took a bite!

"BANK!" the trap snapped shut and caught the little mouse's tail.
"Ouch, the big trap got me!" the big mouse heard him wail.

The trap had snapped his tail right off, and he cried out in pain.
"I'll never, ever look at cheese. I'll never look again."

The old mouse said, "I told you so. Remember what I said?
You're lucky it was just your tail. It could have been your head!"

"…Watch and pray that ye enter not into temptation: the spirit indeed is willing, but the flesh is weak." Matthew 26: 41

SO THE DEVIL'S AFTER YOU? GOOD!

The devil is a busy one.
He never takes a rest.
He knows us humans very well.
And knows what works the best.
And if he's really after you
Count yourself supremely blest!

When you try to hide from him,
Does he always spot you?
Does he always seem too close?
And all the time out-plot you?
If the devil's after you…that's good!
My Friend…
It means he hasn't got you!

:,,,Put on the whole armour of God, that ye may be able to stand against the wiles of the devil. Ephesians 6:11

THE FUR COAT

The cranky bear came stumbling from his chilly winter sleep.
A meeting with his breakfast, now, he fiercely wished to keep..
His twitching nostrils told him that a hunter with a gun
Was hiding very closely. His first instinct was to run…
But wait a bit… perhaps a little bargain could be found.
Without the effort of a chase, perhaps a meeting ground.

"Good day, my friend," the hungry bear said, with a smile.
"Let's not meet in anger. Let's stop and talk a while.
I see you have a noisy gun. What is it that you need?
If we could work together, friend, we could do well indeed."
The hunter hesitated. To talk would do no harm.
"I need a coat of fur today. One that will keep me warm."

The big bear nodded wisely. His voice was soft and sweet.
"My friend, you're very lucky and we're fortunate to meet.
Just come a little closer, let me whisper in your ear.
We both can have the thing we want, but no one else should hear."

The hunter, cold and tired, placed his gun upon the ground
Soon the incident was over, and they hadn't made a sound.

The big bear licked his lips and then he calmly walked away.
No hunger pangs now bothered him… he'd eaten well today.
The hunter was not tired or cold, nor would he ever want for food.
A thick fur coat surrounded him, its fit was very good.

The bear was fully satisfied, and continued with his walking.
When strangers give advice, it's good to understand who's talking.

"…Be sober, Be vigilant, because your adversary, the devil, as a roaring lion (bear?) walketh about, seeking whom he may devour."
I Peter 5:8
(from Grandpa's sermon)

THE BURDEN

The old man bowed beneath his load
While stumbling down the rocky road.

He raised his eyes and looked with dread
A hill before him… up ahead.

A neighbor with his wagon, strong.
Then happen chanced to come along.

He 'whoa-ed' his mules beside the man
Before the rocky hill began.

"Climb aboard the bench, my friend,
I'll take you to your journey's end."

The man was grateful to comply
And settled with a weary sigh.

Renewed his grip upon his pack
That rested on his weary back.

His hands gripped hard his heavy load
And rode the wagon down the road.

The driver, puzzled, shook his head
And finally to the man he said,

"I was so pleased to let you ride,
But why not lay your pack aside?"

"Oh, no, my friend, for I can see
It is enough your mules pull me.

"It's only right I keep my pack
Held firmly high upon my back."

When in due time they reached the town
With heavy pack, the man climbed down.

The mules were tired, for a fact,
As for the man who held the pack
Its weight still rested on his back.

"…Cast all your care upon, for he careth for you." I Peter 5: 7

NOTE: This might remind us of the little boy who rode his stick horse all day, and at evening he complained that he was" just as tired as if he'd walked."

THE DANGEROUS, ROCKY CURVE

He sought a wagon driver and a good, strong team of mules
To cross the mountain daily, pulling wagons carrying grain.
The road that climbed the mountain had a curve, there at the top,
Which was always very dangerous and quite slippery in the rain.

He talked to Henry Johnson, "See that curve, there at the top?
There is that rocky bluff up there? The road goes twisting round.
How near to the edge could your team go before it pitches over?
I don't want my precious grain tossed out upon the ground."

"Oh, Mister, if you give that job to me, you got no worries on your mind.
With my eyes shut, I can drive my mules around that rain-slick ledge.
Why, them old mules of mine have got their feet glued to the ground.
I can take that team, any day'a the week, as close as twelve feet from the edge."

He turned to Jacob Weatherby, "And you, friend? How would you drive?"
Jake said, "Why, I can drive that bloomin' road, day or night, rain or shine!
Yeah, mister, I been drivin' them mules since a'fore the day I learned to talk.
My wagon'll go ten feet from the edge. Shucks, Mister, maybe even nine!"

The third man loudly cleared his throat and smiled. He had his answer ready
"Well Mister, you ain't seen the best'a mules till you see my team a'pullin'.
Them beasts'a mine are strong and steady. Don't you have a fear.
I can drive my team five feet from the edge, and Mister, I ain't foolin'."

With wide and unbelieving eyes, the fourth man looked this way and that.
He opened his mouth and shut it, turning from one man to the other.

"I, too, can haul that load of yours in every kind of beastly weather,
But Mister, that ain't the whole of it, so let me tell you like a brother…

"I know the way that mean old road curves around that slippery mountain side,
But I got'a thing to say to you, Mister… About my drivin, make it plain, man.
I care about my mules and rig, and I care more about my hide.
I promise you I'll take that ornery curve, just as far from the edge of that bluff as I can "

Guess who got the job?

"…Enter not into the path of the wicked, and go not in the way of evil men. Avoid it, pass not by it, turn from it and pass away.
Proverbs 4: 14-15

NOTE: Avoid being close to evil, it might just be contagious.

THE BUILDER'S LAST HOUSE

The millionaire builder had lived a long life
And now, thought to leave work far behind.
He had many carpenters, paying them sell,
The best of the skill he could find.

One special man had been with him for years.
He was careful and sure in his work.
There was never a defect to be overlooked
And never a fault would be found.

This last house would showcase his pride in his work
Like a shining example of pride.
The house would be standing for many a year
Showing beauty, with comfort inside.

The carpenter listened to the old builder's dream
He took in each word that was said.
He had always had hopes for a house of his own
And a bad thought crept inside of his head.

While building this last house, there surely could be
Many ways in a house of that size…
A small thing right here and an omission there
Could be hidden from inspector's eyes.

In this way, he'd have money to build a small house
A roof, sturdy walls, bright paint and such.
Someday, he to, like the builder, could rest
Just a small place… he wouldn't need much.

So a little bit here and a little more there…
And his thieving now made quite a pile.
It would be enough, and his conscious was dulled.
He was content… at least for a while.

A house of this size, only rich men could buy,
Though the windows might let in cold air,
Foundations might shift and the roof beams might sag
But that man could afford the repair.

He nailed the last shingle, brushed on the last paint,
Put a bright, shiny lock on the door.
He tried to escape from the dread of his heart.
For a poor man, he couldn't do more!

With a smile, the rich builder accepted the keys
And held them in his outstretched hand.
The words that he said to the carpenter, then,
Were sounds that the man could not stand.

"This house is for you, for the service you gave,
I know the good work that you do.
During those long years that you worked for me
You were the best worker I knew.

"Your strength and your skill, and your pure honesty
Were a thing that I always admired.
I wish you have this last house that I built,
The last one before I retired."

The carpenter stood there, with the keys in his hand,
No word was he able to speak.
The weight of regret fairly blinded his eyes
And the beat of his heart made him weak.

He watched as the car of the builder drove off,
And a hot tear rolled down his left cheek.

'Whatsoever thy hand findeth to do, do it with thy might…"
Ecclesiastes 9: 10

Also….

"…The bread of deceit is sweet to a man, but afterwards his mouth shall be filled with gravel." Proverbs 20: 17

DOCTOR HOPKINS – YOU CAN FIND ME UP THE STAIR.

A flight of dusty stair steps with an opening on the street,
Doctor Hopkins tapped his scarred cane as he climbed.
His white shirt cuffs were slightly frayed, but coat and tie were neat.
And he rested, as the courthouse timepiece chimed.

His office on the second floor was austere, plain and bare.
At first, he found he could afford no more.
His sign read, "Doctor Hopkins – You can Find Me Up the Stair."
With and an arrow and it pointed t'ward the door.

Time was Doctor Hopkins climbed the steps with youthful ease
And the town folks brought him all their aches and pains.
After office hours, in buggy, with his bag across his knees
He would tend the sick along the country lanes.

There were those who paid with money, other gave him what they could
And the years went whizzing by with lightning speed.
All the babies he delivered grew and left the neighborhood
To secure the homes and jobs that young folks need.

While the fees paid to the doctor often went to pay for pills
That the doctor gave to those who couldn't pay.
He just couldn't find a way to ask the poor to pay their bills
And he thanked God for the strength to rise each day.

Came the time that old Doc Hopkins could not climb the dusty stair,
And he paused and sighed and drew a ragged breath.
He leaned against the grimy wall and offered up a prayer
Then he closed his eyes and waited for his death.

He was carried by his many friends who dressed him his best.
Town folk listened as the final words were said.

Old Doc Hopkins, in the churchyard, finally took a well-earned rest
When they lowered him into his final bed.

The doctor left no money for a marker for his grave.
All he earned, he gave to those in greater need.
For the bills that poor folks could not pay, Doc readily forgave
And he thanked his God that he could do that deed.

Doc's friend, the City Mayor, looked upon the unmarked mound.
How he longed to see a proper carving there.
At the doorway where the doctor died, the city mayor found
What he needed so the mound need not be bare.

The signboard showed an arrow pointing to the stairway door
Telling where the doctor's office would be found.
The mayor ripped the sign away, so proudly then he bore
The arrow sign on to the waiting churchyard ground.

To a pointed stake, the mayor nailed the painted arrow sign
Where the arrow pointed straight up in the air.
Friends and those the doctor helped,
All agreed the sign looked fine.

Pointing up and saying,

DOCTOR HOPKINS - You Can Find Me Up the Stair.

"…Lay not up for yourself treasures on earth, where moth and rust doth corrupt, and where thieves breakthrough and steal.

But lay up for yourselves treasures in heaven, where neither moth nor rust doth corrupt, and where thieves do not break through nor steal."
Matthew 6: 19-20
(from Grandpa's sermons)

THE VOYAGE HOME

The missionary, old and tired, had spent a lifetime of discouragement on a foreign field. Now, he must leave his field of work, for he was made, unwillingly, to yield to home office advice. They said he'd done his duty, God could expect no more, but who can tell? Who knows what God expects when he finally marks the score?

The huge ship plowed through rolling ocean waves to reach home's western shore. The man knelt in his cabin, Bible there beside him, head bowed down to the floor, and he wept for work he'd left undone. He'd needed strength, why was there not a way? He had no one to come home to. He'd given his life to God, what more was there to say?

Then, in his arms he gathered his small belongings and stepped out into the air. He gazed in frank amazement t'ward the strange excitement he saw happening there.

Streamers flew from every pole…noisy crowds were jostling for a better sight. Bands played a lively tune and there had been photos put on billboards left and right. To celebrate the ship's arrival? They really must be carrying home some great celebrity. The missionary, wide-eyed and amazed, thought, "Could someone still remember me?"

Before he could read the banners or come close enough to see the face upon the sign, a movie idol came onto the deck. Autograph seekers quickly formed excited lines. The weary missionary with his burden of unwieldy bags slipped through the mass. On the noisy, crowded deck, no one glanced his way, or stepped aside to let him pass.

He hailed a hired taxicab, and he rode in silence to his lonely room, there he said, "Dear God, please, I need just one small answer before I crawl into this hired bed. I gladly gave my life for You. I did the very best that I could do, gratefully telling others about your great and saving powers, and there is one small thing that bothers…that man who plays a part, the actor, could come home to a joyful, welcoming place. But in that crowd there was no one who even turned to look my way or knew my face."

There, in the silence, in the quiet of the room, he waited for the answer, as he always did. With eyes squeezed tightly closed, he must make certain that his lonely tears were hid. In time the answer came.

"I know your life and I know all the hardships you have met. That actor earned his party, he came home, but, my son, you're not home yet!

"My precious child, you did, in every little way, all that I had in mind for you to do. That party on the dock was NOTHING compared to what is being planned for you."

"…In my father's house are many mansions, if it were not so, I would have told you. I go to prepare a place for you." John 14: 2

"…For as it is written, eye hath not seen, nor ear heard, neither have entered into the heart of man, the things which God hath prepared for them that love him." I Corinthians 2: 9.

(from Grandpa's sermon "You're Not Home Yet.")

LADY ON THE WALL

She knew about them, of course. That wandering
desert tribe.
Their God who gave protecting Power. So hard to
describe…
Though her father tried.

And the camp was close. Why? No one could
conceive.
Perhaps they'll leave.

But they did not. Father sighed and stroked his
beard.
He knew them well. A battle just ahead, her father
feared.
And still they neared.

Safe within those city walls the folks were laughing…
unafraid.
Tall gates. Double thick stone walls. That's why
walls were made.
Father sighed and worked his trade.

Threads of gold to make their shiny girdle stitches.
Silver spoons and knives. Carved vessels, fancy
riches.
Gold for horse's bridle hitches.

Silver lids for bottles made for holding rich perfume.
Rings for ears. Perfect to accentuate a courting
maiden's bloom
Gems. A bride's gift from her groom.

Rahab had long since left her father's house, to climb the wall.
She lived alone. The flags and flax she gathered grew so tall.
She'd dry and sell them all.

She watched the camp… the hovering quiet cloud, and thought…
She turned the drying flax upon her roof. More should be brought
But father told her not.

It was not safe. He knew these wandering people through and through.
Fierce warriors. Naashon led a strong and battle-winning crew.
Often he, whole armies, slew.

A lady with her beauty? Never! Father said, 'not be done'.
But flax? They should be gathered now and spread out to sun.
Should have begun!

Father's silver bracelets, tastefully carved, and still discrete.
Jingling softly, mahing any working lady's gown complete.
Always a worthwhile feat.

A lady on her own must think of more than girdles for her loins.
She must think of value. That's where gold and silver joins.
A girl must eat, and that takes coins.

Peeked through the window.
"But look! See two men come this way.
They move so carefully.
Are they only trying to avoid display?
Or did they chance to stray!

She watched the two men moving…
Artfully through the gate.
Down the stairs she flew.
She had no time to think or wait
And no time for debate!

She, beside them, whispered,
"You must come, and flee.
I'll keep you safe… and help you

see the things you came to see.
Then I'll say what you can do for me."

The startled men, in vain, sought words to make a sensible reply.
But..."Shhh! Don't speak, or I will scream, and if I do, you'll die.
I beg you, quietly comply!"

She, bracelets jingling, whirled and disappeared within the crowd.
What could they do but follow. Their faint hearts pounding loud,
Their bearded faces bowed.

With a fetching smile, a motion of her jewel-fringed shawl,
She slipped within a narrow doorway carved into the city wall.
A step... a stair... a hall...

"You're safe with me. If anyone should see you, you should ask,
'Where is the seller? We would buy her special sun-dried flax.
Say, where are her racks'?"

"But, I saw you come and brought you here for your life's sake.
You'd be quickly known as strangers, at the first word that you spake.
A risk you must not take.

"I know about you... how, out before your army, entire cities fell.
My father told me much. He traveled with you and has much to tell.
Yea, he knows you very well.

"He told me of how Naashon's army razed the wilderness and plain.
Of how they came to Jordan's bank, and turned around again.
He saw it all with shame.

I know these double walls won't stop you. They'll soon be crumbled dust.
I know the people you will slay, and I know why you must.
But I'm one that you can trust.

"I know you'll burn our cities down, but I just don't know how.
I think it might be very soon. I really think it might be now!
So you must vow...

"I saved your life from capture. I knew what I must do.
Now you must save my father's house, for we are part of you.
I will bargain… so, will you?"

There was no time to answer her. Outside the door, a yell.
On the stoop and at the door the stomping footsteps fell.
Frightening, angry voices swell.

A BANG! A CLANG! Strong fists were beating at the door!
Startled eyes within the room. Calm words were said no more.
Dismay… "They'll thoroughly search my floor!"

"Follow me! Climb to the roof. You'll hide among the drying flax.
I've rope and cloth and cutting knives, stored in among the racks.
You'll hide beneath the sacks."

Up the stairs behind her, they all reached the drying room
The flax, the knives, the red, red rope. A linen weaving loom.
A busy, working room.

The locked door burst wide open and soldiers stomped inside.
"The stranger men have disappeared. We're searching far and wide.
We must find where they hide."

Two spies pressed against the floor, into the sacking squeeze.
Flax spores tickle noses but they must never, never sneeze.
Heart quaking with unease.

The lady told the soldiers, "You may search from floor to sky.
I have duties to attend. I have flax to turn and stir, and dry.
You search for your own spy."

They searched inside the cupboard, looked behind the closet door.
Clothing strewed and jewelry flung, then they looked for more.
And her ruffled curtains tore.

They knew two spies had entered and they vainly sought for proof.
Searched from floor to ceiling, missing stairway to the roof.
Left in an outraged huff.

Silence… The door opened.
His feet hesitant of command.
Hoary haired and wizened,
though eyes alert…and sure of hand.
She said, "Father, here they stand."

His faded eyes surveyed the pair,
And looked them through and through.
A nodding of his bearded chin,
"Yes, daughter, these will do."
Then a deep breath drew.

"These people have my history.
Forty years ago we came this way.
We were afraid and faith was weak.
We turned and went away.
I'm truly sad to say.

"Naashon was their leader. He was fierce and firm and fair.
But he must do the people's will and though he sadly saw them err,
He led on, in despair.

"I could not go. With saddened hearts, we bade farewell and stayed.
I HAD to stay. Where people live in houses, there is jewelry to be made.
After all, it is my skill and trade.

"Forty years a stranger. Never to their idols has my own knee bowed.
I knew of your location, from talk about the fire and the moving cloud.
You're my people. I was proud!

"Not a sunrise happened, that I did not think of you.
Not a night I did not dream, and there was nothing I could do.
Someday you would return, my sad heart truly knew.

"I made my bangles, belts and beads and thought about this day.
My daughter's life began. She and the others truly had no say
Where to be born and where to stay.

"And here you stand. Great Nasshon's tall and stalwart son.
My family rescued, thanks to God. And you will be the one
You're here… and it is done."

The spy named Salmon listened to the stooped and wrinkled man.
"To grant your plea, I'm honored. I will do the best I can.
You're one of us, this is your land.

"When you hear the trumpets blow, at time of evening sun,
God will save your daughter's house. You'll be here… everyone.
Our conquest now has just begun."

"In her window, facing west, so our soldiers all will see
Your daughter hangs the red, red rope. That will the signal be
That those within this house are free."

They had to leave. Words from the spies, and bargain made.
"Our life for yours, and utter not word of this our blood-sealed trade,
Watch for us. We will invade."

And with the red, red rope she used to lower bundles down,
She tied to each man, strong, secure, wrapping round and round
Darkness. Then she lowered them without a sound.

The lady watched her neighbors laugh, and tended drying flax.
How soon? She thought, but went about each aimless, useless task.
How soon will come attacks?

Family members, one by one, came to her stone-walled dwelling.
The lady tied her red, red rope to flax, and bundled them for selling.
What the lady knew, she surely was not telling.

The day had come. At rising of the sun they formed their marching line.
Behind the feet of priests who bore the ark, the watched-for sign.
The breeze was clear and fine.

The fighting wanderers crossed the river, stepping up their paces.
While those upon the city wall were laughing in their faces.
Humor in such dangerous places!

In a line they walked. City circled. Then that day they walked away.
For five more days they did the same… silent… never did they stay.
Nor had they words to say.

The seventh day took seven trips around the stone-walled town.
The marchers only looked ahead, the watchers still looked down.
Footsteps… the only sound.

Seven times they circled and stopped when they were through.
Musicians paused and took a breath, with horn to lip, they blew
Among the watchers, apprehension grew.

The blasting of the trumpet sounded piercingly and clear.
Echoes, eerie, floated back, teasing, tormenting every ear.
The sound exciting hidden fear.

Mortar cracked and dust clouds grew, the morning sky was gray.
Rocks, rending, tearing, scraping, falling on the hard-packed clay.
This was indeed the judgment day!

Walls fell flat, and people screamed, as red flames pierced the cloud.
Spitting, crackling, melting, fancy furnishings enshroud.
Cries from within were loud.

By now, the flaming city circled, a crumbled dusty mound.
Homes built-in upon the wall were flattened on the ground.
One house, only, standing sound.

Invaders found the small, wall door, and helped small children out.
They picked they way across hot stones and scattered round about.
Too numb to laugh or shout.

Old grizzled father turned away all help. He would do this alone.
Carefully, securely, moved ahead, avoiding every sizzling stone.
To his God he would atone.

Last to leave the stone-walled house,
Built on the city wall,
Was the jewel-decked lady,
Brave heart pounding, standing tall.
Her courage had arranged it all.

Upon the roof, the sun-dried flax
Cracked in the orange flame.
The racks, the sacking all were gone.
Riches rare of every name.
All ashes were the same.

The scarlet band. Hair piled high
And scarlet kerchief bound.
The smoothest, soft-draped linen.
Her own flax, finest to be found!
The rope with tassels hanging down.

The lady stepped onto the ground.
Not one thing had she forgot.
Around her waist the red, red rope
.... tied tightly, firmly in a knot.
It was appropriate, she thought.

And there. Beside the door, there stood a man. It was great Naashon's son.
The lady nodded, knowing. Father knew the bravest deed was done.
This could truly be the one.

Around them smoldering finery, trash, debris and arid smoke.
It made the eyes burn fiercely, fly ash to make one choke.
No word was ever spoke.

Bracelets dangled on her arm, jeweled combs arranged her hair.
This was a great occasion. Burned in the flame was every care...
She looked ahead... his hand was there.

Hand in hand, they walked along, around each smoking stone.
To a tribe she never knew, and to another, distant home.
But now, she did not walk alone.

The background of this true story is found in the first chapter of Joshua. Rahab, whose father was an Israelite who had journeyed from Egypt, had been expecting this to happen.

Her father, Bezaleel, * had been the maker of the furniture in Gods ark which was carried by the priests wherever the Israelites traveled.

*Exodus 31 gives the background of this man, one of only two men that were given a special occupation. (the other was Shelah who was given skill in linen.) When the Israelites had reached Canaan, they were afraid to go in because the natives were large people. They were turned back into the wilderness for forty years until all the cowards died.

Bezeleel did not go back, but stayed in Jericho. God had told him his work on the ark was finished, so what would a jeweler do in the wilderness? He stayed in Jericho, practicing his skill. His daughter, Rahab, took an 'apartment' on the city wall so she could watch for the return of the Israelite army. When the walls fell, her father, Bezeleel, and all the family were saved.

Rahab married the spy, Salmon, son of the general, Naashon, who presided over the wars in the wilderness. Their son was named, Boaz, who became the father of Obed, who became the father of Jesse, who was the father of David who killed the giant (one of the 'larger' persons of Canaan). God would have known that the Israelites would fail him when they first reached Canaan, so he had a Plan B that consisted of Bezeleel's daughter, Rahab, and her ability to see through the window in the wall.

The account of this linage is found in Matthew 1: 4-6

*Exodus 31: 1-6

ABOUT THE AUTHOR

Joann was born in the mountains of Arkansas in 1933, in the height of the depression, into the family of a pioneer minister. She was attracted to pencils and paper from the time she learned not to poke pencils in her eyes, and that paper did not taste particularly good.

Having an older sister who aspired to be a school teacher, she became a class of one and was expected to master reading at a very early age. Books became the magic that would transport her into another life, and she read and re-read the few that were available until they were limp scraps. It was about then that more stories began to develop within her own head, along with simple rhyming verses. This book is one of the stories.

Her father's occupation as minister, by necessity, put her in church several times a week, where she practically cut her teeth on a church bench, so to speak. There was the small country church that her father built and pastored for years, and later the other churches where he was called, and in that way she became uniquely positioned to meet a lot of people on a regular basis, and appreciate the hard-working settlers who pioneered the land in America's midwest.

This book, and her other books, reflect the lives and attitudes of those of her childhood that she remembers best welded together with a bit of imagination.

CPSIA information can be obtained
at www.ICGtesting.com
Printed in the USA
BVHW071135240521
607998BV00004B/492

9 781649 084774